I LOVE WHALE SHARKS!

By Ruby Stockton

Copyright © 2019 Ruby Stockton

ISBN 978-1-950602-90-2

info@retrogradebooks.com

Rx Books

My name is Ruby. These are my friends A J and Dyllon.

Today we are going to look for

WHALE SHARKS!

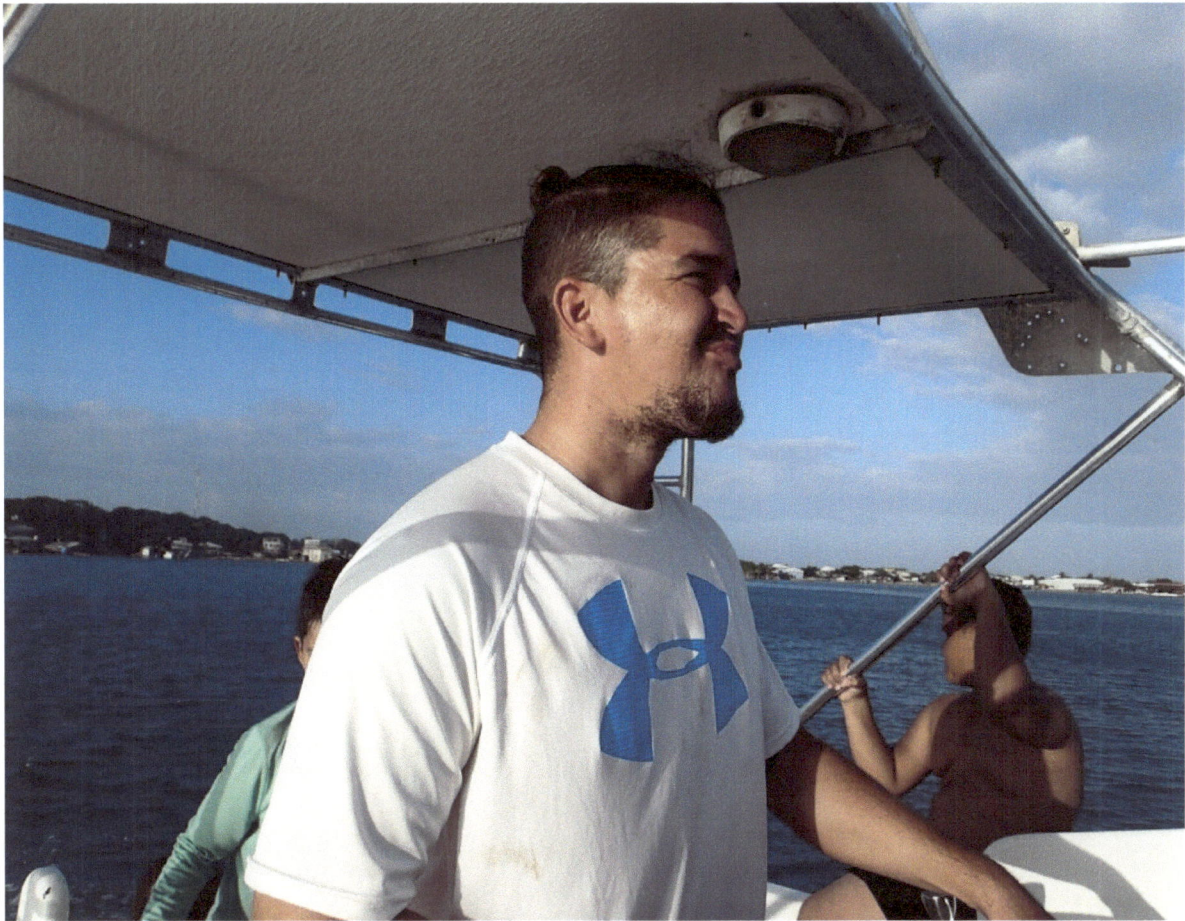

This is our captain. His name is Stanley.

He is the boss of the boat.

Whatever he says, we do!

He keeps us safe.

Today the ocean is calm so he lets us sit with him!

We help him look
out for other boats,
dolphins, turtles
and flying fish.

But mostly we are
looking for signs of
WHALE SHARKS!

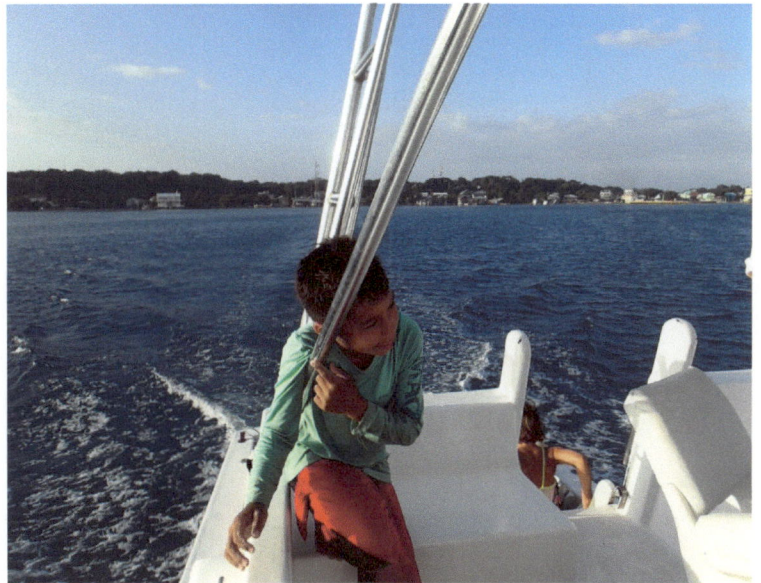

Whale sharks are *sharks* the size of a whale.

SHARK

Gills

Caudal Fin

**Sharks are fish, with skeletons made
from cartilage. They breathe with gills.
Their fin moves back and forth.**

WHALE

Blowhole

Fluke

Whales are mammals, with skeletons made from bones. They breathe with a blowhole. Their fluke moves up and down.

Whale sharks also eat like some whales by filtering *plankton* and small fish with their large mouths and tiny teeth.

Plankton are very tiny plants and animals that float in the water.

To find whale sharks we need to find plankton.

We look for fish boils, where lots of tuna get together to eat plankton and small fish. We also look for birds circling and diving down trying to eat the fish.

From far away it looks like waves on the water.

There is one!

The water looks like it is boiling!

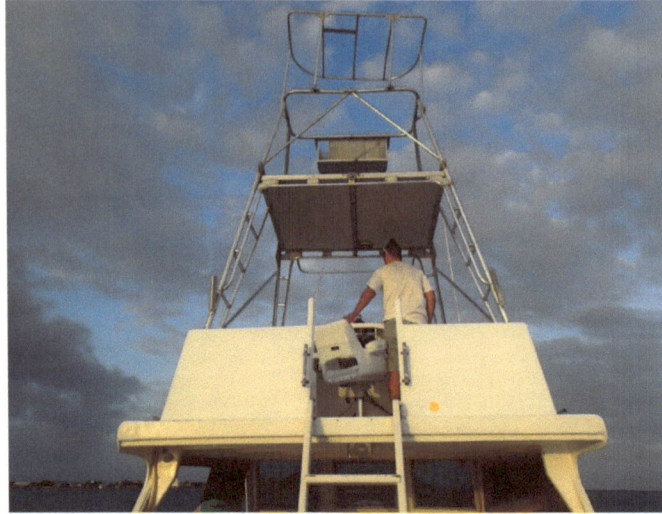

Captain Stanley drives the boat to the boil while we get ready.

This is Andrea. She is our guide.

She helps us get ready.
We need a mask, fins,
and a snorkel.

She tells us the rules.

We must listen to her.

We don't want to scare the

whale shark away!

DO NOT touch a whale shark.

Slide into the water feet first.

Try not to splash.

Listen to the captain.

When the captain says go, GO!

Look down.

When the captain says to come back,
swim back to the boat.

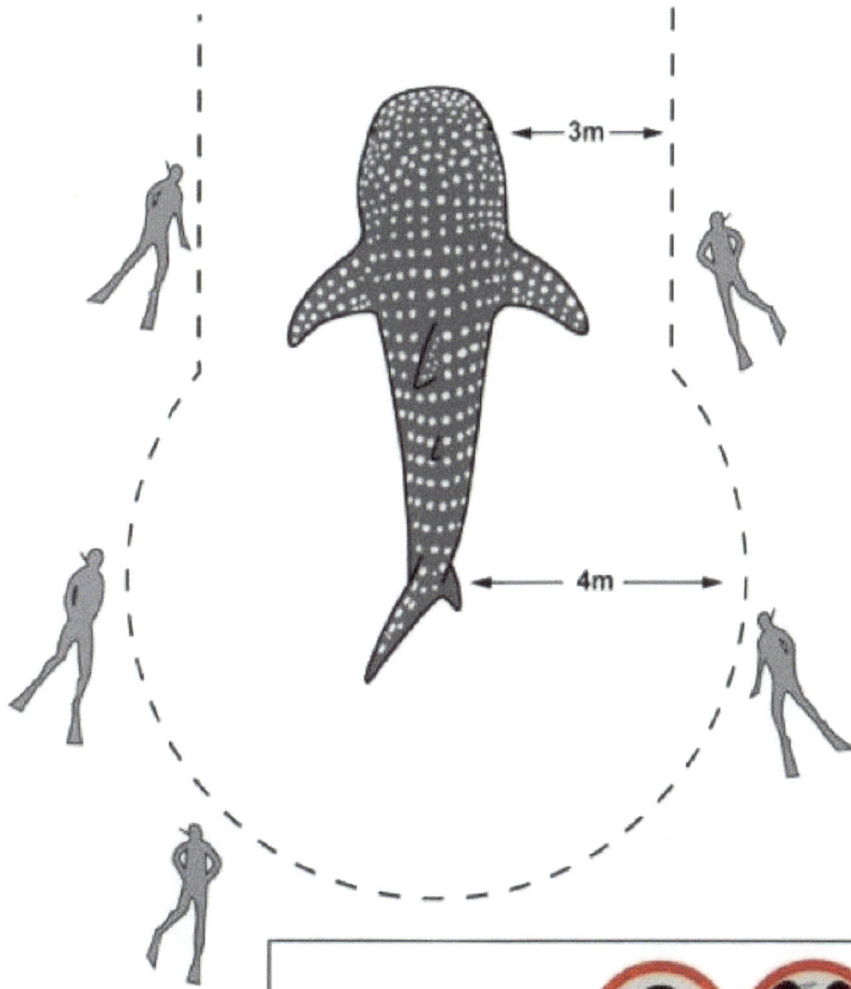

We are almost ready.

Captain Stanley sees the whale shark
swimming near the top of the water.
It looks like a big, dark blob!

He turns the boat and tells Andrea we can get in. GO!

We try not to splash.

We swim and look down.

There it is!

Wow! That was so cool! Did you see its spots?

Did you see how big it was? Did you see its mouth?

It was a little scary but awesome!

The whale shark slowly swims away.

Captain Stanley calls us back to the boat.
We need to get out of the water so another
boat can take a turn.

This is the sign for shark!

We did it! We saw one!

Thank you Captain Stanley and Andrea!

This whale shark was encountered in Utila, Honduras.

Special thanks to Whale Shark Oceanic and Research Center

www.wsorc.org

Thanks to Utila resident Brad Ryon

for photos on cover and pp 8 & 9

MY WHALE SHARK LOG

Date:

Location:

Buddies:

What I Saw:

Picture:

Fun Whale Shark Facts

Whale sharks are called "gentle giants".

Whale sharks have hundreds of tiny teeth!

(smaller than yours!)

Whale sharks' spots are unique like fingerprints.

Scientists use "spot identification" to identify whale sharks.

No one knows where whale sharks go when they are not on the surface yet!

Whale sharks are protected in many countries around the world.

Whale sharks are *ovoviviparous*. That means babies grow in eggs inside their mom but are then born live!

Whale Sharks are Found Near the Equator

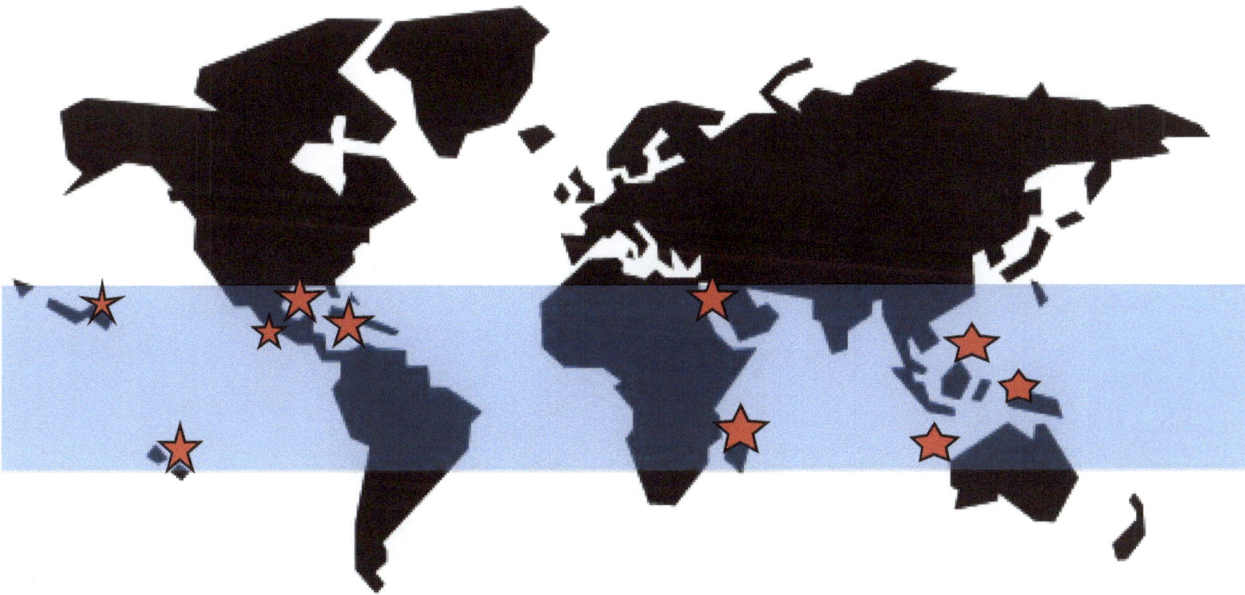

Popular places to see whale sharks in the world:

Utila, Honduras; Donsol, Philippines; Exmouth, Australia; La Paz, Sea of Cortez;

Isla Mujeres, Mexico; Hurghada, Egypt; Galapagos, Ecuador

About the Author

Ruby grew up on the island of Utila, Honduras.

Her favorite activity is snorkeling.

She loves to share the magic of the ocean.

Look for more adventure books by Ruby at
www.retrogradebooks.com/ruby

www.ingramcontent.com/pod-product-compliance
Lightning Source LLC
Chambersburg PA
CBHW060836270326
41933CB00002B/107

9 781950 602902